Poppin' Johnny

POEMS BY

george wallace

ACKNOWLEDGEMENTS
Appreciation to the following publications, in which some of these poems have appeared: *Istanbul Literary Review* (lord of buskers, life goes dead flat in winter, life is not enough); *Writing Outside The Lines* (redhead of my sudden acquaintance; handwriting on the wall); *City Poetry* (i haven't seen her or that dog for years; *Istanbul Review* (since you have told the birds to sing); *Heavy Bear* (some men rub me the wrong way); *bigcitylit* (it's raining again in tinsel town, poppin' johnny); *PPA review* (our planet of sacrificial love); *Gutter Eloquence* (it just chills a man's heart to know); *North Sea Poetry Scene* (too many words); *poetz.com* (i am looking for a hero)

Special thanks to Marvin Bell, Joe Millar, Peter Sears and David St John who helped me in developing this manuscript.

Design: Kat Georges Design, New York
(www.katgeorges.com)

First Edition

ISBN: 978-0-9840700-2-2
Printed in the United States of America

Text set in Bembo Regular 10.5/12.5
with titles in 11.5 pt Bembo Semibold

Published by
Three Rooms Press, New York

www.threeroomspress.blogspot.com
www.myspace.com/threeroomspressms
threeroomspress@mac.com

CONTENTS

Poppin' Johnny

IT'S RAINING AGAIN IN TINSEL TOWN

it's raining again in tinsel town not
unlike port royal in spring & o! i am
having cool drinks with a man who
wears a white slouch hat & looking
like mr moto or only frank o'hara
i'm standing with him under a ceiling
fan life is a black and white movie it's
1942 & he not only knows the customs
agent but what the cargo ships are
carrying on any particular morning
like this morning for example it's
automatic weapons he says jack
daniels too & plenty of it that swill's
much better for a fever than quinine
he says & in fact drunk neat jack is
quite restorative & a necessary item
when you're in the tropics and that's
when he places one hand on my thigh—
life is a gesture, he says, not to say
a luxury, particularly for a man living
on the cheap & with the local economy
being what it is (everybody knows things
have taken a turn for the worse) we all
have to do what we can he says particularly
when there's guerillas (& he begins to sweat
pretty bad like orson welles contemplating a
jackson pollock painting) in the hills i don't mind
i don't really care but if they come to town
let 'em come i mean i always know where to
go in a pinch he says—meaning he keeps
a loaded handgun hidden on a rooftop
behind a cistern in a banana crate

A BUSKERS PRAYER O LORD OF BUSKERS

lord of the buskers
sweet god in your
high grace teach
me the jingle that
makes men jingle
teach me the tune
that makes nickels
wiggle and sing in
the hands of all the
weary souls in the
world in dr gener-
osity's pocket in
the waxy grip of
madame tussaud
o lord of buskers
let the money flow
let the coin fall out
where ever it may
so long as it rolls in
my direction through
every damn hole in
the goddamn world
hole in the bucket
hole in the cloth
hole in the steeple
hole in the skullbone
of enormous heaven
o let it roll into my hand
dear lord of the diminished e
let it roll across my teeth
my tongue my lungs my lips
with vowels like cantaloupes
consonants like spikes like a crown
of thorns hang me on your tree of money
let my throat be filled with middle c's
teach me the sweet notes for
office women who stroll
through city hall park
at lunch with sweet
voices of their own

rolling hips of their own
and lipstick for the office men
in their incredible ill-fitting
suits o lord of buskers
not so much for me
not for me
but for your song
dear lord of vagrants
innocent student of the world
with your magician cap with your
sudden spring and unexpected music
borne into the hearts of women
and men grant me the back beat and the gentle hook
get off your ass, o lord of the mellifluous tune
pluck me a chord six string god
of the strummed guitar
teach me a stray dog blues
a yawp a gypsy warble
oh god of easy smiles
and sweet park benches
send away the cop
on his big ass horse
send me the rich ones
pockets full of expendable
folding money
let's get parisian
about it, you and i!
i mean to hell with eliot
and ezra pound
let my voice be heard
let it rise up like jeremiah
like aznavour or francois villon!
i am your merchant ship
i am your instrument
let your voice rise up
in me and roll on easy
over the high seas
to hong kong
to splitsville
to valparaiso

I'M JUST AN ORDINARY GUY I'M FEELING LIKE PITTSBURGH TONIGHT

i'm just an ordinary guy i'm feeling
like pittsburgh tonight buy me a
beer says choochoo charlie to steel
eyed dick and make it american
he was a little bit older than dick an
old goat a little bit colder to look
at straight in the eye tough old bird
as they say in the rotogravure a
rainboot in a fashion show and also
a little bit

shy what was it they say—he was a
pederaster? a pedophile? he's
never been convicted of nothing
says dick and who are they to judge
anyway both i think knew the truth
of the matter and in an artistic kind
of way there was justice in it they
kept some things to themselves
being men among men

a louder and noisier pair of tools you
won't find in a bag of hammers
they were damn fools in fact they'd
been rolling around this town for
years like a couple of bocci balls on
a poop deck you could say they
were addled you could say they'd
been left a little too long in the sun
or hung out to dry and the truth

be told old steel eye he was the louder
and a whole lot sadder gentleman
of the two six months younger but it
was him who'd actually been to jail
only on trumped up charges but he
learned how to lung a thing out when
it was necessary you could say he
was part thespian he'd been that way
since birth only now it was more

amplified more pure it wasn't exactly
embarrassing and it wasn't cool it
wasn't bad or banal neither in fact
it was a gas to hear them flap their
jaws like that after a day of hard labor
two dudes sitting in box seats as if
they'd paid for them—a couple of
old pigeons in love with the temporary
freedom that nature ordinarily denies

the working man in america when—
what tools some men are in the hands
of fate—the red legs shortstop drops
an easy pop fly the crowd goes wild
and the boys from the home team start
running round the bases like a cork
screw in the monongahela river like
a chevrolet coupe spinning on ice—
ball game over the pirates win

flashbulbs flashing forty six thousand
idiots and change shouting like it was
the fourth of july

STARLIGHT! SO MUCH STARLIGHT!

the late tzarina put some in a snuffbox.
brad pitt poured some onto his cereal.
the candy maker put some of that
good stuff into sugar rock candy.
madam tussaud put some in a wax
museum. so much starlight! like the
governor's aides plotting under a
crystal chandelier. like murder on
a mountaintop. i saw starlight in
the coffins of the mad. i saw
starlight in the eyes of a dog.
i saw a man with a tin badge
he wore starlight on his chest.
handcuffs have it electric lights
have it window shades drawn
at night. everything contains
starlight. the blade of a guillotine.
thunder on the broad plain. starlight
is the first word ever spoken is the first lie
ever told it is the first laughter ever to come
bubbling like milk from a cave. starlight!
we are surrounded by it. filled and
fed on it. bathed in it buried in it.
body parts haddock and chips
marijuana by the ounce
and spearmint chewing gum
all wrapped up in starlight.
fish scales that shimmer and dart
in a quick moving stream
are wrapped in starlight too.
lobster claws. aspirin bottles.
zip loc bags. saxophones and
cigarettes. shook up hipsters
beer bottle drunks letters read and
tossed away. everything is starlight and
that means we are starlight too and therefore
we are made of the same thing everything ever
made is made from—like tinsel angels like crystal meth
like blue crystals in laundry soap. like volcanoes in
their deep lava dream. we are horseflies in

a buzzing stable we are ice cubes in vodka
we are crazed antennae in a radio storm
we are silver coins placed into a beggar's hands.
we are the teenage girl fucked and forgotten and
resurrected. starlight leaks from the mirror in
every public toilet i have ever visited. it's
hung out to dry with the laundry.
it unhinges itself it rubs off on
the bagel maker's hand.
dull as brass doorknobs. shot
by sharpshooters in a penny arcade.
drooling like pigeon shit on the general's
bronze epaulettes. dragonflies. skateboards.
glass eyes. dancing feet. sometimes
when i sneeze the stuff
just comes flying out. some
women's lips pucker in starlight
as they lean forward to kiss a strange man.

THAT GIRL'S A CHEVROLET

she's got celebrity
she's got greed
she's got ammunition
& she's got natural selection
i tell you she's got erudition
palimony free & easy patricide
she's got manifest destiny she's got
motorized magic she's got the tar & feather
thing going on she's the usa she's
easy erection she's got nascar
amputation just look at her
boy she's cocky as a concubine
she's momma's little trailer trash
there she goes boy boom boom
boom! she could rock your socks off
she could take you anywhere
child she could explode at
the slightest provocation
she's off to the races
she's off her rocker
she's not faking it
she's a hustler boy
she's a heartbeat
away from insanity
banging like a bubble
squatting like a bitch
she's out of the showroom
she's out of the confessional
you can't touch a thing like
that & you can't take it home
she's a fortune cookie she's a paper doll
she's got tattoos on both her tits
she's got dancing shoes
on her shapely little rack &
pinion feet she's not a team player,
no sirree! she can't help the way she is
always getting her idiot boyfriend
into the biggest trouble—that
girl's a chevrolet, boy she's
a chevy she's a chevy she's

taking it to the streets
she's talking to herself
she can't stop trying you
on for size—just you look at her!
can't you just about smell it? can't
you just hear it? taste it? right about now
i bet you can feel it in your horny little testicles
i tell you what boy that girl's a chevrolet
she's so helpless she's so vulnerable
she's cute as a button & she's
amenable—what you waiting
for boy! take her for a ride!

CLEAVE UNTO ME

the first time i
saw that goat
footed girl of
mine—cheap
corn crappy
overcooked
dead horse
of a man i
was—well
what could
she possibly
but so what!
i jumped up
kicking like a
frog strapped to
the electric chair
like a quick boy in
a slow schoolyard o
man i wanted her to
cleave unto me right there
in the street more than life
itself i wanted that girl what
a jerk i was she walked by me
angel i said where did you come
from what in heaven is that you are
wearing girl that permeating thing what
the hell is it—she gave me that
particular look of hers—not a
clue what she was looking
for i guess she was just
looking for a guy to
jump out of his
fucking shoes
into love
i can't
say

A MAN ON SKATES

he was an ordinary guy a guy in
a shirt from nine to five with his
bandy legged pants his sleeves
rolled up efficient knowledgeable
about products and parts familiar
with purchasing policies a guy
who you could trust to seal the
deal and not disappear after
lunch or come back high a man
with a grin an ordinary working
stiff from eight to six with bills
to pay little mouths to feed
a dog that needed watering
but on saturday night he put
it all to one side he put all that
away he was a man with a mission
a man who needed to land on mars
or the moon or something a man!
something specific to what he
was before he put away childish
things away before his wife and
his boss and the government began
to tell him who he was supposed to be
a man a man a man he was mad joyful
stupid crazy dangerous impossibly cool
a singleminded determination filled him
bright as two stars mad as static electricity
gulping down deep breath of ice chips
oxygen haze and glinting steel—this
is serious business and man, he was
serious about it! he was fred astaire
pele on skates wily and graceful as a vodka
martini two hours slinking like wily coyote through
arizona cactus fields spinning headlong through
a crowd of teenagers the holy fool he was
a jackrabbit in desert headlights he slid
across the crazy ice rink so damn cool
And surreptitious and infinitely alone
with himself with the elements
hawking girls he could never have

menacing young bucks he could
never beat with his fists at his side
with his jaw stuck out and his elbows
spread out like wings with his style!
his style! no man too fast no woman
too strong nobody was going to stop
him now he forgot who he was for
a little while and the existence of
gravity and the existence of material
circumstances and the existence
of love and rent and work

LIFE GOES DEAD FLAT IN SUMMER

he wants to do it without so much as a whisper. he wants to do it without so much as a blink of the eye. he wants to do it so much! with anyone. with no one. with gene kelly. with himself! he wants to do it so much he could cry. and without a hitch or a care in this world. he wants to hurt someone. hurl a swung bat into the crowd. hit the big one and hit it hard. break into his homerun trot. break out of this damn hole. drink the flask of poison down. wrestle the wreath to the ground. he wants to watch it fall useless onto cobblestones. he wants the world to go round and round and round the flagpole. he wants it to go another round. he wants to be drunk again. every evening at half past eight he wants to enter this bar and empty it. this bar near this place where he met this person he obsessed over for nearly thirteen years. needlessly. he wants to drink at a table by that wall not this one. he wants to sit and think things over. talk to strangers about it and not talk to himself. he wants to listen to the music weave out of and back into the darkness like a bat or a familiar face in a cave. he wants to make faces like jerry lee lewis or like a sleepy bear. he wants to see himself in the mirror. he wants to think about his sister. she wasn't really a drug addict. re: his father he is less sure but what the hell. there's a photo of the man to go on. portly gentleman wearing a brown fedora. he wants to think about a sports trophy in a closet. he wants to think about that high school history teacher with the affected manner and noticeable limp. he wants to think about james dean. he wants to turn down the heat, it goes down hard. he does not want to think about his latest ex-lover. he does not want to think about his mother or how he ought to give her a call. her with her western face like fresh paint or an omelet on a china plate. like a fresh squeezed grapefruit. give that one a call? ask her to explain again why he's a gay man? the sour bitch. no way that's gonna happen! he wants to sit at the piano bar for hours with a napkin and a copy of a french novel. a gold cigarette case in one hand and his forehead in the other. he wants to stir his cocktail with a long graceful finger. he wants to sit alone. to get on with it. get on with it. not get over it. he wants to be gene kelly AND grace kelly. when he stands up he wants to touch the sky. When he sits down he wants to be in the back seat of a hot buick on the road to the poconos. life goes on. life goes on. life goes on.

LIFE IS NOT ENOUGH

life is not enough for some
folks they have to marry it
mob it cheat it eat it they
have to dress it up in white
satin and silk cummerbunds
they have to throw pearls
at life like hail the size of
quail eggs they have to
drink to its soul carry it
in rucksacks bury it in
olive groves wrap it up
in french ribbon trade it
like donkey flesh or skeins
of cloth pluck it like cat gut
pray for it to come back as
wine you see life is just not
good enough for some folks
they have to vote on it write
songs about it lick their left
thumbs and come out fighting
over it they have to organize it
store it stock it love it cross it off
their lists or else catalog it and
leave it to rot on a shelf or possibly
cross themselves with four fingers
cut their front teeth bite on the neck
of life wrestle it to the ground make war
on it you see some folks have to put a spin
on life spit on life or watch life die they have to
tear it up and start all over again you see some people
just can't take life as it is they build churches to life
they tell fortunes with it they peer through it like
a telescope at distant galaxies they roll it up
with cigarette paper and get high on it
some people pick it plant it steal it
hand it over to the authorities
study it like a holy secret or
worship the hell out of it
like the body and blood of
the sons and daughters
who have left them
for lives of their own

BITTEN BY PANDAS

i used to be happy
in my three piece suit
and my petroleum smile
and my four wheel
drive-by all american
cheese machine.
my gas guzzling
whiz-bang she-bop
mommy machine
my spit and shoeshine
pride of ownership
rape of earth machine.
my post modern
job satisfaction
toys for boys
what-a-life, happy!
snuggled down
metrosexual. driving
my time bomb sports
club condominium girl
machine! man alive,
those were the days!
but then i was bitten
by pandas and the greed
went away. and the tyranny
of wishes and the imperiousness of
desire. the pandas stole it all
away and now here's me,
living in trees eating
mollusks on the shore
smoking new bamboo.
here's me, wondering
what's a good american
boy to do after he's been
bitten by pandas?

LIKE MICROBES ON THE FOURTH OF JULY

i feel so cosmic on the fourth of july
or is it election day or memorial day
i forget which but anyhow here i am
standing at the barbecue grill with my
barbecue hat on and my tongs in my hand
and that special sauce with a gal at my side named
sally who and you can quote me on this they
used to call her peaches down at strawberry bottom
but that was back in the day now they don't call her
anything much at all unless she's late for work and
then by god you should hear that fucking phone
ring but anyhow that's my gal sal what i want
to mention is how grateful i am on the fourth
of you know with a six pack of blue ribbon
beer at my side and cooking that good old
chuck steak or maybe it'll be chick fillet
this year and well i'm glad to be alive
and american this year a day off in
the land of the free where a man
can grill whatever he wants to
and be independent about it
and shit and thanks to
all the guys who
made that possible
by dying on our behalf
and also killing other guys
who got in the way of our freedom
and whoever says otherwise can
go to hell and i'm just saying
i'm awfully glad and i am appreciative too and
it makes you think about things like jesus
carrying the cross and nascar and
moses parting the waters and
a microbe named jake
crawling inside the belly of
another microbe named jake
who lives inside a grain of sand
which has no name whatso-
ever it's just a nameless
grain of sand inside

the belly of a microbe named
jake and every damn one
of us are like microbes
crawling around
doing our own thing
being free

RIDING THAT TRAIN TO NEW YORK CITY

i take the train to new york city. the sky
eats everything in its path. trees walls
baby strollers. cinderblocks. bedbugs.
styrofoam. brown whiskey in paper bags.
construction workers. mattresses in big
piles and big plastic wheels. i read in the
papers they're closing coney island down
soon. everything i know is closing down.
everything i know disappears into everything
else i know. like the tunnel of love. like
cigarette smoke disappears into the nostrils
of a woman sitting there idle at a bar on
42nd street. this city has no manners. there's
that smell again, cheap perfume. like grape
fruit rotting in the sun after a long rain. like
harlo in fur. look! everything i know is turned
upside down. an overturned car on fire. a
taxicab. a halo over the baseball stadium.
look! someone has hit a big home run. the
fans are excited. the fans are excited. they're
waving their idiot arms around like it's the big
magic. it isn't the big magic. it's the big panic.
everyone is in it. even the guy sitting next to
me on the train with his mouth hanging wide
open. he's in it too. stupid and capacious man.
slow fool with the eyes of a patsy. he's looking
at his fists and trying to work this thing out.
he's wondering where his money has gone.

THE NEXT BIG TRAIN GOING WEST

after carl sandburg

i sat with a sailor on a bench in a railway station in sandusky ohio in the cold hard midwestern night waiting for the next big train going west. it was a forgotten land, land of utility poles and plenty of cement and the uncovered platform and the trains coming in and out of the yard and it had been snowing pretty hard all night and there was more snow on its way.

I asked him where had he been and he said hong kong. singapore. honolulu. valparaiso. montreal reyjkavik sydney anchorage panama yokahama piraeus port au prince and new york city. he had cruised drunk as the midnight sun through the black waters of the bering strait. he drank so much kava in the south seas until he just couldn't feel his tongue anymore. he had wore grass shoes in mindinao and sunglasses in rio and he'd panhandled for drug money in goa and he had smuggled sapphires west and blue jeans east and he had sat at the feet of a guru in the himalaya foothills.

he had gotten laid in bombay and could speak some arabic and dutch and knew how to handle himself in a barroom brawl and how to tell if a man has a knife.

just then the train from chicago to washington dc our nation's capital came by, carrying loads of men and women in business suits. they had leather briefcases and their overcoats on and most of them were drinking coffee or with their eyes closed or staring at the chicago papers or out the window at us. he asked me where I was from and i said i'm from here, just up the road, vermilion, but i'm headed to any of those places you've been to.

and i asked him where he was headed, and he said cleveland.

HOW IT WORKED

she got up before me every morning at twenty to six
because that was how it worked and i was sleeping in
my clothes again and i was wearing my shoes in bed
which she tolerated and I could smell something
different in the air, not the fresh brewed coffee not her
first morning cigarette (they support each other,
she said, they go together like a woman and a man who
are supposed to support each other support each other)
not the smell of the hot iron which she used every
morning to press her blouse, not the lipstick or the hair
spray she used to hold her pretty hair together—she
put the coffee cup down she tapped me lightly she said
my name real careful real slow real calm and i opened
my eyes pretty fast for a drinking man and then she
kissed me twice and said goodbye—she kissed me
twice and that was not how it worked—and her kiss
didn't taste like her kiss and her face didn't look like her
face, and i laid there like a pizza delivery guy with too
many pizzas to deliver who has fallen off his bicycle and
onto some wet pavement, i laid there like bambi on ice,
like flipper on a plate, and i looked back at her like roy
rogers trying to figure out what is wrong with his faithful
horse trigger—i'm telling you i could feel it, it was
strong, the way she moved her hands, she held her
head sideways like this and smiled at me with more than
the usual smile—and i could just see it in her eyes, a
tremor like southern california, like plate glass in an
empty city on a night when a riot is about to bust—it
was autumn the sun was shining the bedroom curtains
hung there like a jury and i could feel it from my asshole
to my shoes—she was saying goodbye for the last time
—she was going out for the long one

THIS IS FOR THE NIGHTSHIFT GUY

this is for the guy on nightshift who never knew
a minute of financial peace just a working stiff
sweeping it all up gum sticks candy wrappers
and white plastic knives sweeping it all up in
the rich american night penniless as the day
he was born smoking too many cigarettes he
walked the line six nights a week he stayed
a bachelor and he never said boo to nobody
he just walked a sad samba through hallways
and warehouse spaces swaying to the left
swaying to the right crooning like mad sinatra
a broomstick in his tattoo'd arms yes this is for
the nightshift guy i worked with him six weeks
in syracuse ny i hung out with him for three
years after that poor as a mouse scrapmetal
eyes rich one night a week for his whole life
he was nelson fucking rockefeller when saturday
night came around watching the local welterweights
fight drinking tap beer with cubans shouting back
at the cops through the open window saturday
night! it is my champagne he wrote this to his
mother he meant it he eventually woke up on
sunday afternoon wandered through the city
curious about everything this is my beautiful
adopted country he said he was curious as a
river ogling everything in his path trees buildings
war memorial MONY tower the girls in the park
every brick and concrete inch the good life
dear to him as the lump in his throat which
kept on growing the world was his oyster
he laughed it don't bother me none that
is until he went to see the damn doctor
then the rest of the shit went down

THAT'S YOU, MAN

you see that sunshine on the mountaintop? that's you,
man. you see that green and white billboard advertising
newport cigarettes? that's you too. you see the cop in
the rain with the crap blue hat? the hooker with an
armful of dope? that's you. that's you kid holding a
fender guitar in your hands like a secret needle. that's
you running through the streets shouting 'it runs in the
blood it runs in the blood!' that's you the runt of the
litter the jay walking pigeon the mock hotel the cartoon
waitress. that's you in your rock n roll shoes holding
back the flood just because you can. that's you the
biggest goddamn concrete dam east of the mississippi
and that's you the man in the string tie who got a
jumpstart on the blues. that's you in your judge's frock
you the defender of cardboard saints you the bohunk
dieselhair boy. you the irish rover. oh yes that's you kid!
i see you the moonpie in the factory window. i see you
the cranky old bitch wreathed in smoke. i see you in
the all night casino. that's you doing your time in the
tank that's you sitting all alone in the malt shop that's
you eating the best hamburger since the great
depression. see that kid staring into the midway lights?
see that farm boy hopping off the greyhound? you! you
you you! you are sexy as a stick of dynamite you are
tasty as a ballpark wiener you got plenty of mustard on
you. you are stronger than demolition dust you are
happiest when closed before striking you are horniest
when your lungs fill up with high grade petroleum you
are a rain gutter stuffed with leaves you're hundred
dollar bills! that's you in the soup kitchen that's you
in the whole food aisle that's you on the tv you in the info-
mercial you in the spider web that's you in the flapjack
butter you with the hillbilly face walking with one hand
around a factory girl the other hand stuffed in your back
pocket. kid you are no poodle grooming fool you are one
hell of a man both feet in the future three sheets to the
wind bubble busting stoked up number two pencil eating
shit stirring horseflesh trading telephone book tearing
son of a bitch with enormous crab cracking american
jaws. that's you man! that's you! standing in the beat
down doorway of the universe waving back at you!

SO MUCH RAIN

i took the big trip to nowhere there was so much rain
so much rain you know lake fish fell out of the sky there
was rain in my armpits and in my jackboots too there was
rain in the mouth hole of the bill collector there was
rain in the nests of all the bird of prey and on the tin
roofs and trucks delivering milk rain fell in unhappy
buckets there was rain

on the microphone of the speechmakers making their
speeches against war the electric grid was rotten crazy
with rain the cops were too there was rain on the poet
with the perfect smile there was rain gathering in brown
puddles steel girders twisted and danced with rain and
the man in the construction hat with pennies in his
pockets couldn't stop

laughing there was rain on him too and he didn't mind
there was rain so much rain it came out of rich women's
eyes so much rain it came out of the noseholes of saints
so much rain it made the green earth go gray with anger
rain came out of both ends of a holy man it flooded the
midwest i don't know nothing about meteorology and
stuff but i do

know rain when i see it and it sure did rain—so much
rain! like flowers on the little stone marking the grave of
a poet who died in mississippi riding like a damn fool
with the freedom riders

BEFORE EVERYTHING IS OVER

before everything is over i would like to make love to
you the same number of times as a gentleman knocking
on a door that will never open for him.

the same number of times a mirror fails to reflect the
spirit of a ruined man. the same number of times a
young woman discovers in the middle of a noisy party

that she is alone. i would like to make love to you like a
man leaning his face from the window of a passenger
train to catch one more look at the one woman he ever

truly loved but now he regrets leaving behind. like a
circus performer looking up at a ceiling of trapeze rings,
crazy lights and precarious high wires,

knowing he will never climb that high. like a washed up
prize fighter reaching for the canvas because it is his
only friend. like a bum reaching for a twenty dollar bill

that is blowing across a busy boulevard. o i would like to
make love to you before the passersby pass by before
the falling sun falls out of this world

and into the next, before the brown bear of winter falls
into his magnificent winter slumber. i would like to make
love to you with my forehead

pressed to your naked waist. with my platelets pulsing in
your veins. with my brain on fire and snow falling on
your hissing flames. i would like to make

love to you a hundred times with the shuddering
knowledge of you, with your frozen smile and
untraceable fingertips. you with your indecipherable
dreams.

because i am doomed to live with you even when i am without you—you with your incomplete shoulders. you with your rainbow colored lips.

you with your empty hands. your perfumed silence, your perfect elegance. you, with the sunlight that leaks out of your darkness and into my world.

THIS REDHEAD OF MY SUDDEN ACQUAINTANCE

after Neal Cassady

hmmm, well, what i mean to say, the road was
straighter than this, and i was driving unreasonably
fast, a 57 chrysler imperial boy, you remember those, no
of course you don't but oh man, well you know or
maybe you don't, cherry red souped up electric windows
electric top chrome grill big damn fins—but no brakes,
no brakes and you have to scuffle your feet along, take
you three miles to roll, if you want to stop, rocks flying
everywhere and you might need a new pair of
shoes, anyhow I couldn't afford tires, as my situation
concisely speaking was dire if not to say extreme, but
being that it was, i could of course have gone around
the corner, that is to say steal something second
hand, but at the time i was with this redhead of my
sudden acquaintance, well positioned in town, she with
a well oiled boyfriend and me with plenty of time on my
hands but no, he was not in tow on that particular
morning, in fact she had been sitting in a booth at the
diner a very long time by the appearance of things,
coffee cups ashtray full of nervous cigarettes, she was
putting hair pins into and out of her hair, well i struck up
a conversation and it got to be this and it got to be that,
everything was going along pretty damn fine and when i
looked outside as sure as we are sitting here today it
had stopped raining, morning was nearly over, the cat
was out of the bag, so zippity doo! we was off, both of
us shot out of the barrel and that was that, no doubt we
was traveling ten times faster than what is legal, i'm
talking 35 plus 35 plus 35, and then some, and it was
yes man! i mean no not that road outside fort collins i
prefer at this late stage to say it was one of them
back east, headed for her hometown, in kansas, she was
a schoolteacher of good repute you might say, not a cop
car to be seen, the breeze was everything, eastern
colorado was a sight to see, she was smart and
with that orange sky, no not like the red in her hair, a
coppery sort of red like lincoln's pipe on a new shiny

penny, and she gave me the prettiest smile just then,
boy you could just feel it, that car wanted to fly, we
rolled down the windows and beat to the beat on the dash,
oh my, she said, oh my! my right toenail, oh my, i do
believe it has just had an emotion!

MY FIRST DANCE

i walked through a room full of girls like they were
cotton candy like i was a black ant caught in
the folds of a pink carnation remembering
what my mother told me she said
'you're supposed to enjoy yourself george
and behave' but i did not want to behave i wanted to
play hockey like the other boys but i couldn't
play hockey i had to walk up to this
grown man and shake his hand it was an
enormous hand he had fingers like
hot sausages hairy and suspicious and
way too wise in fact his hand was
sweating more than mine that hand was big
as a giant clam the one which was always catching
lloyd bridges by the foot on 'sea hunt' and it wouldn't let
him go and there was old lloyd wreathed in desperate
bubbles and clawing away at his facemask and all that
water and the break for commercial just couldn't
come fast enough for me but eventually i got
away from the man with the sweaty hands
though the girls were still there and
they had terrible smiles and ribbons
stuck in their hair and i tried to loosen my
tie but no luck i couldn't breath and one
of the fat girls pinned me in the
hallway and succeeded in
kissing me and when she was
done with that i went into the kitchen
and i drank a lot of punch from a paper cup
and looked out through the kitchen window to where
the sun was still shining and there was a dog
standing there with his tongue hung out and he was
at the crazy end of a tethered rope he was just trying
to get away from everything he knew in that yard
which was surrounded by a tall fence and all that grass
and when i say grass i mean that yard was covered
with something very much like grass but it wasn't grass
at all in fact the entire yard had been worn down
to nothing but a thin layer of wafer nothingness

just a lot of hard earth and a doghouse
stuck in the middle of it
and plenty of dust everywhere
dust kicked up by the scrabbling
four-legged madness of a dog
who was trying to do nothing more
complicated than just get away.

THEN I KISSED HER

because o it was hot and her lips were
pretty and her mouth opened wide like
a mustard jar and her tongue stuck in
my mouth like feathers in a honey jar
and o her hands and her fingertips too,
palms like flower merchants i kissed her
hands smack smack smack! o what a
perfect gal she was, bottomless as an
oil well olive toned no pit at the center
of her stomach and o she was sweet as
corn bread she was easy as a kitten on
a cross she was not a big bottomed gal
at all, no! and she fell on me like a para-
trooper with no chute on like a six gun
bandito in the blazing sun like hail falls
into willow trees like a plague of frogs
on egyptians like bruises the size of
pigeon eggs like a pirate at his legless
treasure chest and o her sex was like
a corkscrew and her sighs like a coy
little blind little biting thing i kissed her
i kissed her i kissed her! like a farmer
at his plow. like a shepherd at his flock.
i kissed her like a capitalist opening
a bottle of champagne in a formerly
communist country. i kissed her like
a low interest mortgage lender just
trying to get you to take his money.

I IMAGINE YOU NAKED BUT NOT ON SPRING BREAK

i imagine you naked but not on spring break
in a crowd of coeds on a beer keg beach
in fort lauderdale—no! you are naked
at the front door of a hut in the old country
bare feet on cold clay with a stack
of potatoes in the mildewed bedroom
behind you, and a mysterious horseman
riding away over the enormous hill
you are naked behind a haystack
laughing with a springtime of mice
you are naked striding with walt whitman
standing in the sun petaled forest
white skin white as the skins of birches
or in an alpine meadow goatfooted
trying to memorize one of rilke's elegies
or fast asleep on an outcrop of rock
and the salt tongue of the mediterranean
like a sea lizard dancing down at the blue cove
it isn't new orleans no strings of beads
no sultry whirr no overhead fan
no ava gardner suzanne pleshette
no hiding in the attic with your cousin
no back door johnny no test shoot movie no
nineteenth century french pornographer
but in the blue blush of dawn
robe falling away behind you
just took your morning pee
returning to me

YOU WERE A RIVER TO ME ONCE BECAUSE YOU REALLY ARE A RIVER

i loved you once like a fisherman on the edge of a river, with his fingers to his lips, tasting the morning air for salmon. i loved you like a man on a horse entering an undisturbed cove. like a whaler in his scrimshaw dream of hearts and flowers. like a ship's mate who catches first sight of land.

i loved you like a pearl diver below green waves breaking on rocky shoals. like a bear cub at the mouth of his mama's cave with a fresh caught trout in his mouth. i loved you like a prospector, dancing to the sound of radioisotopes in his ears. i loved you like a man with a divining rod in his two fists.

like a willow branch thrumming to the sound of pure undisturbed underground water. i loved you like a hunter examining his plaid shirt for holes. i loved you like a mole sleeping under new mown grass. i loved you like a firefighter entering a room full of smoke loves the children trapped inside that room.

i loved you like an old man in front of his little plate of stewed prunes, whose eyes are open wide as the sea.

you were a river to me once because you really are a river. i did not know what a river could do but then i found out.

I SAW YOU THROUGH THE WINDOW OF A CROSS-TOWN BUS

sometimes i wonder if nature is
through fucking with me
i mean if i was meant to be
cooped up like this in
a cross town bus
after spending all day
in front of a computer screen
crunching numbers i might as well be
back in a one room hovel in
eastern fucking europe listening to
other eastern fucking europeans argue over
a fucking chicken and anyhow leaning my head
like this against a bus window leaning my
head against a paper thin wall or staring at
the ceiling of my shitty apartment in brooklyn
listening to air conditioners harmonize what's
the difference or should i say standing on a corner
of asphalt paradise with these bad shoes on
a cup of american coffee in one hand
and a new york fucking post in
the other—i want to
shout out 'no more
contact with the world!
make way for the skyscrapers!'
and after all why not let's strip away
the last root and remnant of manhattan island
let's make way for subway cars full
of dumbfucking straphangers
give me steam pipes streetlights and manhole
covers no feet no spore no
shovel of breath
no welcome air no frog
no shale no croaking pond no
lily pad or fish spawn to
distract me take away
every spare molecule
of earth fill my mouth with
ashes and paychecks
full of empty lies make of me
a human engine

to your urban design
but then i saw
you, through the window
of a bus on the eighth street crosstown line,
stopping to examine a shop display
on christopher street

I FELL IN LOVE HER NAME WAS EDDIE

i fell in love her name was eddie, life was good for six months life was good. in winter we threw bread crusts into the snow and watched the sparrows fighting over them. when summer came we slept naked in front of a rotating fan.

then eddie got a good job working for a local vet, me i took this job steaming bagels. i dreamed about having a son who would play football and maybe go to the university and get a big job in the city. i never could guess what eddie dreamed about exactly.

but like i say after six months she was gone—eddie ran off with the dogfood guy. i stayed on right here, setting up bagels for the morning crowd—landscapers, school teachers, lobster trap boys, nurses getting off shift or going on, local cops, sunday morning insomniacs

and the bastards in expensive suits with twelve minutes left to catch the commuter train to town.

OUR LADIES OF THE LAUNDROMAT

sitting on three folding metal chairs out front during break
in summer when sun bleaches the cracked sidewalk
in spring when the air's soft and their hair's gathered up
into three perfect little knots and with children playing in
the back and even in winter with its easy accents and

dark eyes and snowclouds piled up like cream filled
wedding cakes and they've been folding sheets and
pillowcases all day—rolled socks men's underwear
shirts shirts shirts bath towels and an occasional lady's
blouse still warm from the dryer—folding and stacking

laundry all day someone else's laundry on a stainless
steel counter and they're shy about things and curious
at the same time with their secret smiles and complicated
ambitions and three sets of hands in their laps patiently
folded up and they don't look at me until i've walked past

and they don't expect that they've been noticed by anyone at all,
nobody exactly, three laundromat gals taking three small self
contained sips of coke from three coke cans and hiding three
perfect rows of uncomplicated teeth and their laughter, their
laughter, like many rifles firing from a village far far away

DAYDREAMING MAGELLAN

you can't ever be totally positive about such things. in
the land of the reincarnated that boy walking slowly
through the grocery store

aisles rearranging cereal boxes might be a daydreaming
magellan. in the land of the reincarnated, the shelf
stocker may have taught

chekhov his grammar. that checkout girl with the blank
stare? she could be helen of troy. you can't be too sure
you can't be too

sure. you never know who's handling your aubergines.
just to be on the safe side, when the boys in the pickle
aisle get to talking

amongst themselves, it would not be unwise to stop look
and listen. the kid with the mop in his hand may have
built violins in cremona.

NIGHT BASEBALL

sitting in the nosebleed seats thinking about nothing in particular
on any given night a couple of dozen nights a year me and fifty
thousand other guys we love the same team the same team the same
damn team we loved them last year when they came in third and
we are going to love them this year win or lose we will groan when
the other team scores we will go wild when our boys win—

go ahead and laugh but the place flips out when we goddamn win
it i mean it's summertime it's hot in the city where else is there to
go the plumbers the electricians the short order cooks the poolroom
jokers we are all here automotive part delivery men junkbond
salesmen cops and crooks and gals who drive yellow cabs you name
it marginally employed men women and children of america

fifty thousand of us strong hopeful and resilient every one of us
pounding the same fist into the same leather imaginary mitt hoping
an easy pop-up or hot grounder or foul tip comes our way heads
up crack the bat sharing this great american city sharing this fine
heartbeat of it all the nosebleed seats the nosebleed seats man i
mean i would cut you off in a new york minute to get

through traffic and i know you wouldn't blink if i was lying there
on the hot anonymous street so ok we can agree on that but we can
put aside our differences for a couple of hours because we are not
out in the street we are in the stadium we are gathered here together
to enjoy night baseball we are comrades in arms sitting high above
the only game in town we share it we cheer it we go

crazy together no threat of thunderstorm no triple digit heat no
muggings in the park no pink slip can keep us away we are in love
with the emerald field the rosin in the bag the dark clean beautiful
night shimmering like fruitbats in the sky a jet passes overhead an
orange moon rises like a pumpkin over left field the whole world a
world away we are in the one place we can agree to love—in the

ballpark the world smells sweet as hotdogs we are shoulder to
shoulder swinging for the stands bleachered out slogging our beer
and cotton candy the aroma the taste the ocean of it all moving like
a wave the big cheer sitting up in the third deck or along the first
base line night after baseball night and the game tastes like a good
cigar smoked out in the open air angelic mysterious and fine

we love the game we love the game and we love the same team our
boys in pinstripes rookie shortstops who field like cinderella old
timers who can barely bend their knees hardnosed boys and fancy
stars washed up pitchers moping in the bullpen and the utility dude
on the bench playing out his option we even love the manager with
his tantrums and excuses and the third base coach who

windmills the lead runner home the crackerjack man the organ
player and the moron who keeps shouting 'hey you big fat slob'
when the cleanup guy from the other team strides to the plate he
stretches his arms he is a pumped up dude stoked on steroids he
can't swallow or chew gum —evil slugger for the other team he is
wreathed in malevolent pride—ugly from his nostrils to his toes

when he swings the bat he can crush a fastball like bones we hate
that man we want our bastard to strike their bastard out

WE PASS EACH OTHER IN SUNFLOWER DAY

though two eyes only have traveled your path—
path of storms storm of books books of winter winter
of the heart—though two eyes only have traveled your
road—calypso road hipster road four wheel road wreck
crossing incredible american rain soaked
road of rusted wheat—

everywhere you look, the simple beautiful farmlands
being harvested—and you tightening your belt your
midwest slurring of speech—your ballfield of prayer
your faltering line drive caught in mid-air—bell
ringing in the misty great lake—trousers
sagging like a sailor in

a drunken alleyway—a footnote in history like a fool
in a tuxedo or a hurricane over the atlantic dying out
or veering toward open sea before it can make landfall—
o saint of near misses o heart of my heart opening up
in the chill before dawn on the wine-soaked
embarcadero—o child

with noisy toys and terrible hair waking me up innocent
in your play—o secret butterfly on my lapel—you are
news to me, news from abroad always about to arrive you
are lost postcard, visionary hollywood—everything always
turning everything arriving departing—everything i've
ever seen disappears—

love closing down like an ice cream shop on the beach
shuttered against the wind—just a page from yesterday's
news—everything comes to life and flies and falters like a
bird that flies beyond itself before falling—my icarus—my
big fat canary of love at the end of your big fat life—crazy as
a traffic light in a jackson

pollock shitstorm—flame bright the moment before it dies—third eye opening—autumn sun coming up—we pass each other in sunflower day—we greet each other and pass—o sudden hypnosis of the heart! o hip gone ghostkeeper of mine! ghostkeeper of autumn! ghostkeeper of my golden dawn!

IT JUST CHILLS A MAN'S HEART TO KNOW

there's nothing i like better than a working man's bar
at four thirty in the afternoon when there's no one
supposed to be there but there you are anyway and
fuck the boss with his big fat hemorrhoid of a mouth
and his paycheck eyes if he says anything tomorrow
after a day like the one you just had today, such as
where the hell were you yesterday at four thirty in the
afternoon, there'll be hell to pay, hell to pay! i tell you
however there's no hell to pay in this joint and if you
want to know the truth it just chills a man's heart to
know that even in the worst of circumstances, there's
always a working man's bar with no one in it and you
can sit there with a beer in your left hand and your
money in your right and no one not a single solitary soul
in the universe is going to say a word about it

HOW MEN DRINK

my father was a bartender and i have been a drinking
man so i know some things about drinking and let me
tell you son some men drink like a busted fire hydrant
some men drink like a rag doll in the pouring rain some
men drink like a river that refuses to remain a river
and some like a fire truck that wants to put out a fire

some men drink like they are mad to live and others like
they insist on dying others like the are afraid to. some
men drink like a liar or a politician who is punishing his
own tongue. some men drink like a surgeon who does
not trust his own hands and some men drink like a
cliché that wants to be an original

my father was a bartender and i have been a drinking
man so I know some things and let me tell you son the
sky drinks from the earth and the ocean drinks from the
clouds. when you reach for the bottle be careful you
don't grab your own ass.

how do i drink? sometimes i drink like a barrel cactus in
the desert other times i drink like a circus act just pulled
into town

some men drink like skin and bones some men drink like
they are knee deep some men drink like the last cheerio
in the cereal bowl and others like a frog in a wishing well
some men drink like a bedstain that cannot be washed
clean some men drink to find their way home and some
men drink to kill the memory of home.

some men drink like a cat from an open container of
milk some men drink like a crack in a porcelain cup
some men drink like a hole in the bottom of a bitter sea
some men drink like a herd of cattle being driven to
market and some men drink like a white tail deer under
nameless stars

i knew a man who drank a bottle of bourbon a day and
he loved his wife until the day he died.

i also knew a man who drank like a coward with a gun in
his hand and the hollow dawn approaching

FRIEND OF THE DEVIL

riding in the back of a panel truck thinking about lilac bushes up north instead of the job i was on which was building those damn hearing booths for doctor offices in chapel hill or raleigh which chris and me well i shouldn't complain we used to do that from time to time i'd say maybe three of them a month which was good money back in those days we must've made oh between a hundred and

a hundred twenty five dollars between us it kept us out of trouble with the wives who were always wanting us to work and normally happy to see us rolling home at the end of the day flush with rent money and we didn't mind it much and it was good money good money i tell you we were young studs we were out there on the big american highway coming home from somewhere

important like mebane or wadesboro or even winston-salem i believe one time it was charlotte like i say i can't remember all the places we used to build those damn things but at the end of the day with the sun setting real soft on the skin of the known world and chris starting in with his singing he especially liked the grateful dead it just got to me, i was happy, that's all,

i will confess it now there were times i would even pluck up a gut and sing along with him, until that is when he started in on friend of the devil which i didn't go for that kind of sentiment back in those days so i'd change the subject and yell out something stupid like look! a couple of deer! and chris would smile at me because he knew there wasn't no deer out there whatsoever

but he would look out to where i was pointing, out into the thick dark woods of north carolina ripping past us at a million miles an hour, and he'd stop his singing and say i think i saw them too

I LIKE TO DRIVE YOU AFTER MIDNIGHT, BQE

i like to drive you after midnight bqe
when the panel trucks are all
gone when the kosciuszko
bridge when graffiti watchtower
when domino sugar when rooftops
and secret apertures of night
gazing into red brick apartments
when the last stragglers from manhattan
a day's hard devotion to the pursuit of
money are gone! all locked up! clear sailing tonight!
o how the skyline rises up to greet me
fdr williamsburg downtown uptown
empire state madison square
grand central bleecker bowery the whole
shit and caboodle of new york city
sandcastles built on the impossible shore of
negro graveyards and old dutch bones
fat and famous glamorous false
men with pride men with sex
and money money money money
a continent of money
turtle island money
hudson river palisades
jersey city meadowlands
half past ts eliot
whore on a
bedsheet
american money
shameless money
i knock you out
i lay you down
i put you behind me
strung out sea to shining
sardine dock and saltine cracker
slipping past slipping by
slipping on home to
you, where you will be
sitting at the kitchen table

with a skyline of bills
waiting for me
and wondering
which one should i
pay tonight the milkman or
the electric meter

TO LEARN HOW TO LIVE WITHOUT WORK

to learn how to live
without work
sit very quietly
outside your door
with the porch light
doused, the clock radio off
and your two hands
in your lap—those
two hands i mean, which
no longer belong to
you—and sit very quietly,
before the milk truck
of dawn can disturb things,
before the first ambulance
of day can rescue people from
each other—the damaged
ones, the compliant and the useful,
the unsatisfied and the damned—look!
daylight creeps up and conquers night.
listen! a tree wren is chirping for its
mate in the unkempt branches
of a crabapple tree.
get down on your knees.
taste the dew rising in uncut grass.
consider the heartbeat of the earth,
rich with sunlight and undisturbed prayer.
the prairie is growing up around
you. hoofprints! mouse scat!
grouse on the wing!
beneath your grateful hands
the grassland—at last!—
has returned
to seed.

RIGHT SQUARE IN THE MIDDLE OF IT

quarter to three terminal d
dallas fort worth airport mac-
donalds i got half an hour to kill
my plane's taking off for
oklahoma city
in half an hour—half
an hour to kill—
i should be thinking about this
thing i'll be doing in okla-
homa instead i've sat myself down
right square in the middle of things and i'm
thinking about a kid in a t-shirt
womping spacerats
on a video machine
in the terminal
with his dad
who's wearing
a pink ralph lauren
golf shirt and
smiling with his perfect
blonde texas teeth
and his perfect blond texas hair
and well the boy looks
just like the dad and the dad
looks just like the boy
and just now the boy has womped
hisself a spacerat good
yeeee haw! shouts the boy
yeeeeee haw!
he's womped a rat
that boy must've learned
to shout yeeeee haw like that
from his dad—i purse my lips
i shape my mouth
y'haw y'haw
it doesn't come out right
now it's dad's turn
at the video game
and it's only a matter
of seconds before he's shouting

yeeee haw! yeeee haw!
he has womped hisself a rat too
there are airports
in every city
there are macdonalds
in every town
but sure as shooting
there is only one place
in this world
where a boy
and a man
can yell
yeeee haw
exactly like that
and here i've
gone and sat myself down
right square in the middle of it

TOKAY & RICE-A-RONI

we were poor but we were also young & innocent &
wanting to experience the west. that old green ford from
her uncle in philadelphia didn't run so good but we
made san francisco in six days & left it to die in a
parking lot. in the morning the bay was pretty for kites
& some people had some kids & let them play around in
the rocks & empty bottles.

we did pretty much what we wanted, on a clear day you
could see sausalito or oakland & understand how jack
london lived there once & there was plenty of land. for
example you could ride across the golden gate to marin
through a tunnel with a rainbow painted on it—i heard
there was redwoods up there, but we never saw them—
also you could catch a bus south

to the coastal range with the pacific fog piling up like a
fifty car collision on the I-5 the air was salty &
eucalyptus to the tongue even where you could drink
coffee & look at seals on a rock yawping like walt
whitman in a wet black robe at his high school
graduation. did i mention sage brush on the cliffs? she'd
walk steep and shortlegged like she was yosemite sam

the cartoon cowboy & me with blazing imaginary six
guns & a big floppy hat on, chasing bugs bunny through
gold prospecting country. not much work back then
& the mission district was a bitch. we were surrounded
by desperate people foolish sometimes shooting up in an
alley or else waving a luger at you for money & selfish
though she had a friend in the castro district

who was high on love & sometimes good for some cash.
but sometimes we were flush & those were the good
times, especially when i sold blood or got a day job at a
factory by getting up early standing on line with winos &
other restless dudes & raising my hand when they called
out my name. on those days i'd stop for a beer & if i had
money left bring it home. we'd buy tokay & rice-a-roni.

she'd cook it up while i sat there at the kitchen table drinking in the late afternoon sun. i just kind of enjoyed watching that rice-a-roni dance & jump around in the cast iron skillet like moths in a fire. like ranch hands doing a do-si-do with some pretty women they had miraculously found in town on a saturday night. big boned women wearing earrings & silver bracelets, who those ranch hands

were bound & determined to hang onto for a few hours & show a good time to.

I WALKED DOWNTOWN TO THE DOCKS AT DAWN

i walked downtown to the docks at dawn
to drink beer and listen to the news of
the men at the fish market; men who have
been up for hours hauling in nets and fixing
crab pots and loading and unloading crates of
fresh fish— mackerel flounder seabass and fluke;
shrimp packed in ice, red snapper and hake;
men who will walk with you unevenly on
cobblestones in big dutch boots who spit
salt water and bite down hard on pipe stems;
men who unwrap sticks of chewing gum
and shove it into their tombstone mouths and
they offer you a piece and mean it and you
really need to take it; men who hide their
smiles behind thin blonde beards
who wrestle and play dice at the bar
who sling crushed ice at each other
for fun; large men and small and
there are a couple of odd women
at the bar too in mud spat boots
and their hands are big as a pair of
lobster claws; big as the hands
of a brown bear who has been
fishing in a cold stream in autumn
and has just caught himself a salmon;
men who hose down fins scales blood
guts and bones of fish every day of their
lives at dawn and they do not care they do
not care they just wash their hands of work
and go drown out the sound of morning traffic
with cold beer and music and pickled eggs.

MAKE A MEADOW IN THE WORLD

if it is cows, they will clang like
church bells on a sunday morning,
and their bodies will turn shut like a
barn door against the rain. if it is sheep,
they will stare at you in the driving snow,
like you are an alien spaceship and they are
extras in a spielberg film. if your meadow
is as small as a child's left hand, mind-horses
will gallop in it and flying squirrels populate its cartoon
sky. if it is ass sideways against the salty atlantic,
seagulls will find a field of boulders to smash
clams against. make a meadow somewhere
in the world that cannot be undone by law or by profit,
a meadow that cannot be sold off. a meadow
nobody can own completely, including
yourself. make a meadow, protect it from
politicians and real estate agents,
and then ignore it for awhile.
before long, pheasants will prowl
the eastern border, silver fox will trot
across it. a bull will paw the furious dust
in august and make your children laugh.
someone will fly a kite or set off a bottle rocket.
a neighbor will mow the grass, when it has grown
too tall to walk through, for summer hay.
make a meadow. it doesn't matter if it stretches
all the way to the state highway or to china.
it doesn't matter if it meanders for a hundred yards
down by the river or is as wide as heaven in some spots.
it doesn't matter if it is square and tight and penurious
as an envelope to tithe in or if it goes cross grain
to the sun or follows orion's knife into the
northern horizon. make a meadow in the world
where there was no meadow before. then,
make a covenant with your meadow,
to never sell it off or to build anything useful
on it. if you do that, before long
there will be a moose
standing in the middle of it,
expressing his gratitude

as only a moose knows how,
antler deep and moo'ing
like an evening train
in the pond weed
and the sweet
tasting water lilies.

EVERYTHING IS GOING TO BE OKAY

everything is going to be
okay. crickets will sing
for you. maple leaves
will turn their maple leaf
colors. northern mists
will descend from canada
to cool things down. the
terrible winds will subside.
it'll be october and the
hurricanes will be over.
okay i will not be here
but everything is going
to be all right. the sky
will open up its arms
again and embrace you,
the way summer held you
in its strong arms. the way
winter tends to grip the world
in snow but then it lets the world go.
the way sunlight held you like a yellow
daffodil in green grass in spring. before you
met me, i mean, before i held your hand
in my hand. the way the memory of
my hand in yours will hold you,
after i am gone. all the long
years you will go on living
in this world, without me.

I HAVEN'T SEEN HER OR THAT DOG IN YEARS

we used to sit in the warm morning sun on a couch in
winter with no clothes on eating slices of apple and
farmers cheese the dog half asleep on the floor a
brewed pot of tea a platter of fresh baked bread early
tangerines with no pits in them bitter to the taste with
an inner sweetness and several sections of the sunday
paper tossed every which way

like a pile of leaves blown from the tops of trees we
used to sit there in the warm morning sun for hours
doing nothing naked as the skin of unstained furniture
wood brilliant and content listening to the news that old
wooden frame house of hers creaking in the winter sun,
morning ticktocking across the window and the radio on
the radio on

and sometimes we made love right there on the
hardwood floor with the dust bunnies and the cobwebs
and potted plants fashion section of the newspaper
under her left shoulder and the sports section pressed
against her butt and the dog didn't every raise an
eyebrow but now i'm standing in the back of a deli with
a ten spot in my hand and nowhere to go

there's rain in the forecast i haven't seen her or that dog
in years

i used to think she was so very smart so very smart and
beautiful too with her eyes very smart and beautiful
pretty hair and beautiful smile smart look in those eyes
and sensitive too—sensitive as a clam or an oyster she
knew how to hold her knowledge in she knew how to
turn a grain of sand into a pearl

yes she was a precious thing she was a precious thing
only a person who could figure out how to get inside her
could get inside her because you see you couldn't just
possess her you couldn't just pry her open with the flat
side of a knife you couldn't just smash her open on a
rock you couldn't just nuzzle her open like the nose end
of a curious dog

you couldn't just run her over with a ten ton truck

only the warm sunny soup of love could ever get her to
open up

I AM LOOKING FOR A HERO

america i am looking for a hero who i can look up to
a hero who can stand on his two hind legs
a hero who knows how to pick his fights
who knows who he's fighting for and why he's fighting
and loves the people he's fighting for
more than he loves his fists or his face
more than he loves the sound of his own voice

i am looking for a hero who is not a hyena
a hero who can admit it when he's wrong
a real live hero not the cartoon kind
not the campaign kind or the football kind
no apologists or bigot or braggarts
no country club grinners no gun-toting fools
no radio rabid mouthpiece men

a hero who can get up in the morning
and break open a pair of eggs and fry them
and wash his face in a prairie stream
and look himself straight in the eye
eyes like a pair of circling hawks
circling each other in the enormous sky
with mud on his heels and a chin like a silver dollar
chin like a monument chin like an escarpment

a hero to save the farm and unhand nell!
face down the evil forecloser!
with his whiplash shoes
his whiplash sneer
with his whiplash cape
with his damaged skin
and banker's hands
a hero who will stand up to the evildoers
who growl at the widow and tie her to the tracks

no limbaugh in his talk show armchair
no limbaugh in his easy sneer
with his get out of my way!
get out of my way!
their right to plunder their right to win

their right to take and bulldoze and bully and toss away
mouthpiece of thieves! conservator of greed!
who steals from the people and feathers their nest?
who smirk and laughs and waves their flag?
who walks across the bones of the weak
the hardworking the lame
the homeless the poor?

i am looking for a hero
who will stand up for justice
not just the freedom part
let justice ring with freedom too!
in the name of free enterprise
in the name of the constitution
in the name of the american dream
freedom to blunder! freedom to take!
freedom to dig from the land and to not put back
freedom to redistribute into their own hands
and to gut-snatch the tundra
in the name of oil

i am looking for a hero
with a chin like a mountain chain
eyebrows like wild goats
ears like mountain streams
and a couple of mountain climbers
with their ropes and cleats
climbing along with them
no chow me down no watch me work
no gator up or eat this sucker
no schwartzenator
no set in the helicopter seat
no shoot us up some arctic wolves
a hero in his chaps and jeans
a hero in his birkenstock shoes

dang i shouldna et them hotdogs
dang i shouldna killed them injuns
dang i shouldna stole that land

WHY THEY FOUGHT

they fought because they were poor
they fought because they were obedient
they fought because they were fooled by their leaders
they were bored or adventurous or cruel or unkind
they thought their families needed to be saved
or their nation needed protecting
or their way of life or their god
they fought against the others
and the fighting was good
it ennobled them
it elevated their masters
it covered them in rich blood
it got them out of the sticky hole
they had been thrust into
it wiped the enemy off the map
it expanded the power of their nation
they fought, and it took something away from them
which everyone said they needed to lose

SHE REMINDED ME OF MY MATEWAN DAYS

with a tongue rough as coal
busted up knuckled under
crooked as a willow
timber faced sulfured out
she reminded me
of my matewan days
fed by a filthy culvert
smeared and yellowed
marched along unceremonious-like
after the harlan shootouts
no diamonds in these hills
no gold in the green flowing river
lost as a bucket in a blue star mine
a collapsed lung like a nest of
naked hairless baby mice
in each dying hand

BOOKS LIKE HANDCUFFS

i found her in bed with them, books like handcuffs
she begged for them sometimes and i was only human
i was only being kind i gave her books the soft
covered type with their keen eyes and their seductive
coughing the hardbound kind too sprawled across her
duvet like stiffnecked soldiers, spines like bayonets,
she wanted books books books she wanted books like a
dumbwaiter wants tray after tray of the blue plate
special like a mountain climber wants a rockfaced
mountain to climb books like whips books like chains
books like spanish olives she wanted to be stuffed with
them and i was her man i gave her more books than she
could possibly handle an avalanche of them they began
to fall like delicate ferns like alpine flowers—before long
i had buried her up to her pretty neck in them

SHE IS THROUGH WITH MEN & THE BELLYACHES THEY GIVE HER

she is through with men & the bellyaches they give her,
the continuing saga of them, men & their machines, the
saints among them, sinners martyrs & thieves, the
wrongs they do each other, the self-inflicted wounds,
the unplanned sacrifices, men with blisters & unholy
smells, poker faced & hotdiggety, naked ambitious men,
broke legs & bottled up with fear, their unbending
demands, men telling unkind truths, their big feet
tucked up under the dinner table, their crooked smiles
she is through with men and their blemishes, the
unspeakable philanderings they think they can hide,
their bony knees that poke through trousers, their
clumsy hands in bed their boyish grimaces balancing
acts & unnecessary lies, their half eaten sandwiches,
mama's boys & solo flyers, explorers accountants &
empty hearts, unshaved, bald or graying men, urgent
whisperers, men with secret animus, men in old
underwear, mechanically disinclined, hollywood dropout,
empty suited bunched up in a corner men, through with
their uneasy promises, through with their drill bits &
sudden poetry, through the monuments they build to
each other, through with men men men men men! him
especially! until the next one

OUR PLANET OF SACRIFICIAL LOVE

sun fell in love with darkness
   and the dark fell in love right back.

but being opposites they could not
   touch each other.

therefore earth was born so the two of them
   could have a place to meet.

this makes any object which throws a shadow
   an agent of their love.

this makes any object which can be put to flames
   an agent of their love.

earth, our planet of sacrificial love.

rock. river. truckstop. parking lot.
   wildcat. textile mill. tophat. corncob pipe.

apartment house. suspension bridge.
   goat. cathedral. christmas tree.

a man with a shovel like me.

THEY TOOK THEM AWAY
THEY SWAPPED THEM OUT

they took them away
they took their names away
they took them away
the fireman in his bed of smoke
the dream model
the hotel conciérge
the namibian attaché
they disappeared them
they did not leave us any receipt
they took them away
the park avenue madam
in her six figure fur coat
the clammer with black-strap molasses eyes
the son of a special prosecutor
an aide to the governor
the child who refused to speak
the dead of night unruly children of america
they made no promises they took them away
they took them away they swapped them out
servants of the industrial machine
silk manufacturers and insurance salesmen
traffic cops and madison avenue pretzel vendors
they took them away their eyes like polished wood
they took away their identity papers
hobos under the ramp of the BQE
smokers of deadly wishes
jokers in the funeral procession
immigrant girls in the cardboard factory
ballroom dancers under the dumb music of stars
they took them away the midnight willows
weeping like a train they took them away in their
volvos and their buy americans
ivy league heroes with big money in their pockets
panicked whisperers in the small hours before dawn
with their faces made up like gift eggs by fabergé
with their hands that resemble mothers' eager hands
the fifth grade teacher in high heel sneakers scoring
coke the shirt launderer with his fuzzy promises and
eager good will peace demonstrators nuclear physicists
railway conductors psychologists with their pills and

goodnight kisses auto parts men drunk on ice hockey
and bottled belgian beer they took them away
they did not offer any explanation
hipsters in the park brains buzzing with ancient jazz
car mechanics with grease in their honest hair
office girls with their legs like fireproof steel
men who drink the wall street cocktail
women who steal hearts for a living
who stare out a window
who stare at a newspaper
who close their eyes and see the future
who imagine swimming in the polluted river
who imagine viva las vegas who imagine nothing
they took them away standing up at the national anthem
they took them away seated at the negotiation table
while the amber streetlights were shining
while we looked the other way
they took them away
they took them away
and they made room for the others

THE WOODS WE USED TO RUN

now they've put another row of split level houses in
the woods we used to run.

i'm talking all along the stony crest of woodhull road and
down through the hollow where there was a stream and
salamanders when it was spring.

you could find snowdrops creeping up through the ivy
and the dead oak leaves along the crest and if you
walked down in that hollow you'd get your shoes wet in
no time flat.

those trees were huge to us then and one summer we
built a beaver dam and watched that stream swell up
into a lake. that was johnny troviato's idea, he had a bb
gun and an allowance and wasn't afraid to use either of
them.

one winter there was a bum in the snow smoking and
drinking from a bottle and sitting in front of a lean-to on
a log in front of a fire. we sat with him for a long time
even though i didn't want to.

he didn't make a lot of sense to me but someone said he
had been to the war and furthermore had seen chicago.

SINCE YOU HAVE TOLD THE BIRDS TO SING

since you have told the birds to sing have them rise
for us too have them blot out the sky with their angry
breath have them darken the wind with their crazy
wings and strange cries—and since you have told

the flowers to rise have them cover the earth for us
have them ruin the meadows with their soft sweet
petals and their unruly pollen have them cast their
children out like criminals into the world have them

eat the wind whole have them swallow the sun have
them walk like apostles into the stinging rain—and
since you have told the worms to crawl into the fat
bellies of men and the wolves to hunt for the weak

and the elderly and since you have told tumbleweeds
to run away from each other and the crabs in the sea
to wave their arms like scissors—and since you have
told the horses to race along and the dogs to bark

and scorpions to sting and since you have told lizards
to bask in the heat and since you have told elephants
to clown with each other and the mountain trout and
the cinch bugs and the cottonwoods down by the river –

and since you have told the people to fight with each
Other and to kill or be killed and to hunger for each
other and fear and make claim, have them love each
other too—have them feed have them clothe have

them shelter have them nurse have them love each
other anyway—and when they're done with all that
tell them to sing to each other too, for us

IT IS THANKSGIVING WHERE ARE THE INDIANS?

it is thanksgiving i ought to thank someone but where
are the indians? i put my coat on i walk out into the frost
i put my feet to the ground like an indian i step out into
the cold as if i have deerskin moccasins on. i walk down
to a place in the woods with a stream in it that you
and i dammed up like a couple of beaver one year for fun.

listen! that's the sound of nobody getting into their cars.
that's the sound of nobody hurting anyone this time.
that's the sound of people who are asleep in their beds,
a people who for one moment are not busy trying to
own the land. it is the sound of women who were
patient with their men and men who were patient with
their women right back.

and horses that did not bridle and men who bought each
other beer and women who loved each other gracefully
and parents who died knowing their children loved
them. it is the sound of a child who will discover love as
if it is the first love and the voice of god in her ear as if
it is the only god. it is the sound of a beaver dam

holding the water back. it is thanksgiving and morning is
quiet as an Indian trail. i would like to thank the silent
people who sharpened their tools and did their work and
saw their fortunes rise and fall and their paychecks
come and go and their kids come and go too and they
passed it all on without complaining. people who were wise

people who were foolish people who were innocent in
their hearts and lived to tell it and people who were loud
and with big fists but they used their big voices to speak
truth and their fists to reach out against power gone
wrong. i would like to thank all the people who knew
when it was time to place their hands at their sides and let

a cheap shot slide. i would like to thank the leaves for falling so quietly from the trees. it is thanksgiving i look out past the bare trees and out over suburban rooftops and further than that, out to the city. so many people! you are out there with them like indians under their wet blanket of earth but i don't know where. i would like to thank you too.

WALT WHITMAN MAKES LOVE TO HIS WHEELBARROW

we slept 'til ten but then we got up & we went outside & we found old walt alone in the carriage shed behind the fancy place on ryerson street. it was brooklyn he had bought that place for his mother with eighteen hundred forty dollars cash (it was the building boom back then & he'd been doing very well for himself) & there he was bare-chested as a summer pumpkin & to be honest with you he was humping that wheelbarrow like an insurance salesman who has taken his girl to the jersey shore for the very first time & wants to show her a real good time —well & we didn't know which way to look! he had that barrow spread-eagled atop a keg of near beer & there they were going at it like no man's business—a large man, old walt, even then, large in the chest, his eyes wild & green as a new pickle but his legs were thin & white as locomotive smoke. white as white chickens.

SOME MEN RUB ME THE WRONG WAY

some men rub me the wrong way i mean knew a man who was so small if you blinked too fast you might miss him entirely. i knew another guy awkwarder than a tadpole in a tea cup and another guy who kept saying how smart he was and how he was in the war. another guy told me he used to play the saxophone on television for money.

some men could go twenty-two years without looking at themselves in a mirror and other men won't change their socks until the basketball season ends but it is usually their appetites that bug me—men with appetites for pain men with appetites for domination.

leather shoes! imported beer! tits like tomatoes! tongues like cigar kisses!

free checking! hotdogs for a nickel! couches with holes!

backpedaling on a promise faster than pigs on ice!

some men are a cardiologist's wet dream some men are disrespectful to their subordinates some men dance like a toaster in a tub and have shocking bits of hair.

have you ever seen a man walk into a bar at dusk alone? walk back out several hours later as sober and alone as when he went in, out into the new fallen snow? have you ever seen a man on a subway unsteady on his feet or avoiding eye contact or trying to fold a newspaper under his chin?

some men could take a woman out on a date and fall asleep on a restaurant plate. some men are like a telephone call home only they've reversed the charges. some men have an appetite for girls that wiggle like vincent van gogh or moonbeams on a small harbor with nothing but a soft breeze to disturb the night.

some men could shoot a pocket watch out of the sky blindfolded if they had an ak-47 and i know a man who is remarkable in every way he could probably run for the governor of illinois.

i respect a man who is like a parachute over a lake of fire.

but honestly some men are like little boys who never wake up 'til half past half way home.

A WOMAN GOES SHOPPING

a woman is wanted for purchasing bread and milk from
a bay ridge convenience shop using a credit card which
did not belong to her.

a woman was observed through security cameras in the
bathroom of a stop & shop with a ten pound turkey
pressed between her thighs.

a mount olive woman removed peaches from a grocer
who had fruit lined up in boxes along the sidewalk in
front of his store.

a cape girardeau mother of three was detained by
security personnel after being observed cramming two
new york strip steaks, four rib-eyes, three hams and a
pound of cheddar cheese into her purse.

a grocery thief with a ham in tow was chased three
blocks before being apprehended. a pork roast bandit
in a gray hat and blue jeans escaped with the loot under
her coat. a san diego grocery clerk was repeatedly
stabbed by a known food thief.

a serial thief who was stopped by undercover police in
the meat aisle of a fort worth supermarket and resisted
arrest was shot and killed.

an elderly woman grabbed a pineapple and grapes from
an upper east side grocery store at lexington and 96th.
she then stole a knitted hat off a man's head and put it
on to disguise herself and run away.

TOO MANY WORDS

too many words cross the boulevard
without looking both ways. too many words
enter the recruiting station with
empty hands and come out carrying a gun.
too many words leave their sons and
daughters behind or their parents
or their wives or husbands.
too many words
sit in front of a television screen
watching the twentyfour hour news for
twentyfour hours. too many words stuff a duffel bag
with fists of sand. too many words go blind.
too many words come home without
their legs on, without their helmets
on, come home without their
buddies or their minds.
too many words stay at home
and write about things they don't understand.
too many words die crossing a desert
that never asked to be crossed.

SHOPGIRLS

shopgirls at the sales counter shopgirls in the aisles
shopgirls waxed washed turned on walking arm in arm
with coffee—shopgirls hips like snowplows breasts like
battleships hair piled up like a parade of 19th

century prussian officers with square shoulders big faced
leggy girls hot as artillery feet like little soldiers tripped
out schoolgirls earning a few extra bucks lips like cherry
pies armed with slicing knife tongues

like a string of christmas lights moody eyed beaten
down plate glass window girls eyeliner freckles
hyperactive hypnotized frightened hymnal girls in
salvation army frocks girls on the prowl girls in twos and
threes

waiting all day for santa santa santa santa mallrats from
eastern europe central america and staten island girls
checking out the checkout line bloomingdale girls
cosmetics girls perfume haired blue smock lipstick

microwave crockpot rosewater big hankie customer
complaint form girls! girls! girls! shopgirls! spinning
down the aisle like fluorescent cotton candy

SONGS ABOUT MY INCREDIBLE EXPERIENCES

looking back on it i must have didn't want that check for
one hundred thirty seven nineteen a week all that bad
especially after a couple of months punching in and all
day long having to eat their and i mean total lack of
respect and what, a half hour for

lunch? under a fluorescent—hey you can't make this
shit up—bulb? and then punch out again, me and all
the other suckers file out of the building and there's
them in their executive parking lot with country club hair
and sports collars smoking their

cigarettes right down to their cash happy smirking
faces and laughing at the rest of us so i said to one of
them hey if you want something to laugh at well you can
hoist this right up your ass well it got back to my boss
and of course he started in on me

like you wouldn't believe and things got worse from
there i mean he started pushing me around like a two
dollar whore and me i pushed him right back like he was
a fat man on ice skates and well you can believe i got
the better part of the exchange but

obviously I had to quit on the place before they fired me
okay? but so what i've been living like this for a year you
see how things are on this side it's not much but not so
bad not so bad at all it's like being a college kid not too
much to lose not so far to fall

whereas when the entire deck of shit happy cards comes
tumbling down on their miserable republican asses
they'll be sorry as hell won't they while I won't be sorry
at all and i might just learn to play guitar and make up
songs about my incredible experiences

i mean just think about it if that isn't a perfectly
honorable way to live then i don't know what and
anyhow like the good book says poverty sucks but
working for the devil is much much worser

STUCK IN TRAFFIC LISTENING TO THE NEWS

stuck in traffic listening to the news told every 22
minutes i am trying to imagine what i thought it was
supposed to mean to me. flapjacks orange juice coffee
all morning lying in my flannel bed a fat newspaper fat
as a newborn child fat as a bag of paper money and a
fat contented sky full of last night's wine buzzing
between my ears. local politics at the annual barbecue
firemen shaking hands with bespectacled councilmen
introducing themselves to each other hair dressers i
used to think i wanted to fuck but now i know better.
dogs with no leashes rakes with wooden handles shovels
and mowers and stacked wood stacked three seasons
high and seasoned with black widow spiders and
cobwebs in the woodshed.

bicycle wheels baseball cards and 7-elevens. odd dog
barking or a car backfiring through the neighborhood at
3 a.m. full moons quarter moons no moons. beach rocks
and whelk sacs drying on the sill. high school teachers
moonlighting in new car sales. grandma olive at her
window talking to the ashes of her dead husband gone
these fifteen years. teenage boys loud and leggy in the
pizza parlor. business men business women standing at
the smart commuter station wearing black leather gloves
and city overcoats collars tucked up to their ears. old
man van alt with leaves and lanolin in his hair explaining
that what you're looking at here is the very last sheep
anywhere between cold spring and setauket.

I KNOW A DWARF WHEN I SEE ONE

i know a dwarf when i see one and i tell you that wasn't
no dwarf it was just an ordinary fiddle player at the
general store a fiddle player that's all with a bluegrass
jug band no not the skinny one on the standup bass
one of them three or four squat ones he wasn't no dwarf
and besides who cares they were all wearing hillbilly
hats and overalls and a'plonking their instruments
like they were apple-bobbing under the stars which of
course we were not under the stars we were indoors
in front of a plywood two-by-four stage and the boys
they played so reasonably well a lot of texas twosteps
country waltzes and hinky-dinky hillbilly songs all
dancing tunes and performed with tolerable enthusiasm
everyone familiar with everybody and all dressed up for
dancing and hair slicked down for the men and the
ladies with their hair done up and their skirts tucked
under and everybody twirling around the men tying their
partners up into little dancing knots that kept untying
themselves and the women making little eddies out of
themselves like there was a good eating trout below the
surface of their ponds but in the bobbed up numbers
everybody got to dancing like they were headed in no
particular direction they just dieseled themselves up
more individually and popping around on the dance floor
like moths in a frying pan up and down they went their
arms at their sides and clickity-clacking and throwing out
of feet in radical directions and their chins pointed this
way that way someplace only they could see invisible to
anyone but themselves, not quite heaven and not quite
hell who can tell for sure these days but i mean hey!
they danced like a bunch of them wooden doll puppets
you put on a flat slab of shingle and bounce up and
down on your knee whittled up wood puppets of good
white pine with loose dowels at the hips so the legs just
go out in all miscellaneous directions they danced like
that, but not me! sitting with a couple of the older
fellas the ones too crazy to dance the maddest old boys
in the county with wiry no account moonshine faces
whitebearded and blue huckleberry eyes fresh duck
feathers in their hair fishhooks tucked in their hats

and one of them i swear had an earthworm still on it,
wriggling it wasn't the grand old opry but there was ice
cream and candy in open barrels and soda pop and
leather goods and fancy cowboy hats on racks all
wholesome and scrubbed up and polite and decent and i
tell you once the dancers hit the floor it was a sight to
see some of them were pretty damn good at it, a lot of
them not so much so but one or two had this thing
worked out to a science and could turn a graceful move
excellent and unconcerned and not of this world not of
this world and smiles on their faces unlike how they look
when you see them at work or at church
it was a brushed up innocent bittersweet jug band
saturday night dancing like sugar in the hollow it was
good as any old thing you've ever seen a human do on
two legs, including figure skating in the olympics or
running from a bear or being chased by a hive of angry
bees which and i can testify to it you know i ran like that
once i was sixteen we was out in the woods but it wasn't
bees at all, just someone i was attempting to avoid a
fellow and i forget who that one time soaked a hanging
rope in gasoline and he lit it up and he swung it around
and it caught fire to my hair it took several days for my
momma to get that damn smell of gasoline out my head
and they had to cut my hair off to do it so i know
whereof i speak and i know that wasn't no dwarf

OH HOW HEAVENLY

to hang around with
portia branningate
at the starbucks
downtown
with her
painted nails
& her brown leggy
hair—she has
a smile like brancusi—
i know a nice set
of tits when
i see them &
portia's got em.
how beautiful to sit
& drink coffee
with a good woman
like that & listen to her
do that college talk with
her perfectly pretty mouth
like a city drowned in louisiana.
poverty, she says, is killing hope.
we have to end some war somewhere.
then there's this foreign boy she sits next to in
chem class & he snores. politics!
i don't know shit about it
but i do know this,
there are no wrong words
when you're in love
& it is summer & i could
listen to portia branningate all day
& anyhow portia is twenty & i
am almost seventeen so

i'm in love with her
& i am going to
kiss her

I LOVE YOU, YOU ARE LIKE AMERICA

i love you, you are like america
and when you talk from one side
of your mouth you are huck finn
on a raft you are a playground
swing in dampening wind you are
a hobo on a sad shining road a
mayfly a mustard stain a hot dog
stand a sweet crazy grace note
a spring flower on a hot day
a city with a pulse a goldmine
that just won't quit and when you
talk from the other side of your
mouth you are like america too
a herd of buffalo in sleet a mallard
duck in a small muddy creek a tomboy
with a twisted braid a slide trombone
that has lost its way you are a ball
game at night bases loaded nobody
out you are goldenrod and i am sure
i love you from both sides of my heart
and from the soles of my feet i am sure—
but then you start in talking from both
sides of your mouth again and the bed
room walls begin to shrink the wallpaper
starts to peel and you are fighterjets
taking off before dawn you are share
croppers sullen cops lynch mobs bill
collectors—you are ampules of dust
in a thousand broken alleyways you
are a government of one a factory that
doesn't sleep you are a conveyor belt
that won't convey you are a dull machine
that devours its young and spits out
the bones and then from both sides of
my heart and from the soles of my feet
i'm just not sure how i feel about anything
anymore—not you not me not america.

YOU MIGHT BE DINNER

i love you truly dear and enter you the way a worm
enters an overripe peach the way a bear cub enters a
mother bear's cave the way a salmon, weary with
the sea, enters the mouth of the river where he was
born

but you may be a punching bag for marsupials a charity
fuck for a hedgehog a midday treat for an owl you may
be a hitch hike ride to a dandelion seed the laughing
stock of angels dinner to a crab

o servant of the weak o temple of the greater gods o
marvelous carbon dioxide maker from the moment i laid
hands upon you from the moment i called you mine like
a stray cloud to hurricanes like a landing pad for fleas
like a dust bunny to a roc i have loved you truly dear

but you may be
a signpost for migrating birds

THE HANDWRITING ON THE WALL

i see how the boys look at each other when the boss
walks past and sally looks nervous at the end of her shift
standing on line at the bus stop in front of the bank
waiting for the number eleven downtown which will take
her from that waitress job which even with tips and
kissing ass it doesn't cover the cost of rent gas groceries
and electric not to mention a babysitter which you have
to have one to even go to work in the first place and she
probably makes more than you do, and baby formula
too

and i see how the deli clerk goes deaf dumb and blind
after the other guys have been let go and he's the last
guy pulling in a paycheck and he's got to get that
macaroni cooked and serve it too and the shrinking
mounds of egg salad and potato salad and the long line
at the counter of working men and women with no
expressions on their faces they don't much look at each
other just at the headlines in the papers or down at their
own shoes on someone else's floor and go back to their
own deep thoughts

i see how the newspapers shrink and they stop telling
the news and the headlines are all about crimes and
accidents and celebrities i never even heard of and
scores to games i never even watched and they try to
get us to hate each other instead of them because
someone figured out that if the people know the real
score they'll take it to the streets and then there'll be
real trouble

and if there's real trouble the cops'll be in the streets
again with their billyclubs and their tear gas and their
nightsticks

and even though the little kids still walk hand in hand
through the park to school and they don't even know
that times are hard and unfair they just draw their
breath in the winter air and they see it when it comes
out again all misted up and looking pretty and real good
their own breath in their own thin air it makes them
laugh and giggle and want to do it more

and even though my hands are too cold in my gloves to
flex and unflex them and the car won't crank and i
couldn't work a job for decent pay even if there was one
because my old bones couldn't stand it and even though
i hear people say it's been like this before and the
country got through it that time and we'll get through it
again somehow and fuck the rich people and the
powerful anyway because rich people always get away
with it until the greed is exposed and the
fingerpointing's done and the bastards get their due
and when things settle down there's new rich people
and powerful to take their place

and anyhow in hard times the common decency of the
american people is not only restored but it will prevail
the rough and tumble spirit of the american people will
carry us through

i can still see the handwriting on the wall

I AM A NATION AT WAR WITH ITSELF

i am a nation at war with itself. i am a veteran with a beret and a bad heart and war memorial eyes and life is a kind of death and peace is a kind of war. peace is a kind of hunger. desire is a kind of hatred. and i am a cut flower in a blue vase on a tabletop in a country kitchen. and i admire your hands.

the way you move your hands on the table top. the way you handle a butcher's knife. with your tongue like a roasted red pepper. with your eyes like garlic cloves. with your voice in the deepest candlelight making love to the night. like a power plant makes love to the dead ukraine.

light is a kind of darkness and i am a black bird in the night. and i am one with the people in your darkness and i am not blind. i am not blind! i can see what's what. and you with all the people on your enemy list. you with your endless armies of young men to slaughter and to waste.

i am a gospel church on sunday and music is a kind of silence. i am a nurse in a hospital tent exhausted and no more supplies. and compassion is a kind of cruelty and silence is complicity and money is a kind of poverty in the soup kitchen of your heart. and i am a lentil bean floating in your soup.

NEW WORLD LOVE SONG

o i am a paint pot
o i am a clay pipe
o i am a pint of grog
o i am a tar pit deep
in the mouth of a man
i am a plug of tobacco
i climb into hell and out again
with a silver spoon in my neck
o i am hercules with the smallpox
i am on a sacred mission from god
i make love to a thousand women a day and then
i fall asleep like a housecat in a holocaust
and o i do love their mouths and i do love
their hair and their breasts and their
eyes and their linen and o i do love
my own mouth too because it makes me feel
holier than thou it makes me feel like
peter stuyvesant or maybe peter
the great and o i am a fur trader on
the mohawk river i have plenty of rifles
i have plenty of firewater i have
hard candy for the pretty ladies
i have a blanket of fleas for my own
true wife and o when i cradle my rifle
in my arms i am an egg-laying
son of a bitch on the banks
of the fucking ohio
and when i cradle my
woman in my arms
i am a conquistador
in the heart of the desert
and when i make love
to my wife it is like
a weathervane
spinning in a hurricane
and when i am not making love
to my wife i am making love to a continent
i am breaking bread with the angels
i am walking in the promised
land and o my love she is

a grove of almond trees
she is exotic she
climbs like a
gypsy waggon
climbs into the
andalucian sky and o
after kissing my woman
on her lips and on her sweet
breasts i do not want to make love
to a thousand women a day
and o i cannot wash that taste
of her away because
she tastes like fresh chalk
she tastes like a blackboard
she tastes like a convent
like a dogfish
like honeybees
like wheat
like turnips
like depleted uranium

she tastes like gun metal
she tastes like an inland sea

LIKE CHARLES REZNIKOFF IN THE RAIN

i keep leaving the factory but
the factory keeps following me
home the factory keeps keeping
pace with me like a conveyor belt
crooning its ordinary song in rusty
brooklyn dark like a door to door
salesman selling pots and pans under
a cottonwood tree like summernights
stammering with stung leaves of steel
the factory the factory the factory in
every streetlight lamp lamp lamp like
jimmy durante singing missus calabash
to sleep right there behind me two steps
from oblivion one step from the precious
light like charles reznikoff in the rain with
his dull hat pulled down over his ears his
vaudevillean eyes re-examining every line
break in this poem o! dreary as third base
dreary out tonight, tonight is just a night
like every night isn't it mr reznikoff i am
a good citizen too all day long i stamp
out communists all night i dream your
heart of hearts comes back to life—
beating on my pillow just now like
a stunned rabbit in the grass

YOUR FACE

your chin like a fire
escape your eyes like
a jailbird behind rusty
bars your ears waiting
for lights out & the dark
whispering your tongue
like bukowski at the race
track reaching into empty
pockets for a pencil your
eyebrows like steve mcqueen
& those movie germans
your hair like a college
kid high on lsd your
cheeks like a small
town in a twister in
central iowa your
mouth like a monkey
did i mention your
nose with its pleasant
ancestry? your
face your face
like picasso on a
bicycle like a
black cat in
the pouring rain—
like a coconut
falling from a
coconut tree

A FOUR DOLLAR MISTAKE

i took a girl to a movie i think orlando
bloom was in it & bought her a bag of buttered
popcorn even though i knew perfectly

well it was a four dollar mistake because
it wasn't popcorn she was after (& me neither)
but no doubt me. all the way home

she let me hold her sticky hand
in my own sticky hand.

WORKING OFF THE JACK

all the time in the world telling
a mess of those damn lies again
tino been working off the jack
been shooting off his big mouth
like a kid with a bb gun smoking
that sage brush just a man with
a machine he's been busting up
concrete think he's heavy action
captain kirk think he's blasting
aliens in the oleander—star wars
cupid in chains the accidental
alphabet well everybody knows
he's not & especially in the a.m.
& that bug-eyed old lady of his
staring back at him like a leaky
old pickup with a busted radiator
parked at the foot of his bed

I MADE A WISH LIST AND YOU WEREN'T ON IT

i made a wish list and you weren't on it i wished for all
the good things money can buy and an island of my own
to enjoy them on and i was glad you weren't there to
ruin things for me with your poormouth poetry

i loved that little island of mine i loved yoga class and
backyard barbecues i loved art openings and the best
bargains in town i loved hundreds of delicatessens and
foreign film miracle miles ballroom dancing and neighbors

my little island in the lukewarm sun a billion houses on it
but the people i shared it with didn't bother me like you
bother me and when i walked along the asphalt roads in
spring i could still find nature on it, real nature—

the lawns grew great happy moptops of wild onion grass
and when the pear cactus bloomed yellow blossoms on
the beach in summer i didn't touch the spines and in the
fall when an ocean of oak leaves rustled under my feet
i kicked the leaves mightily

like a kid on the way to reluctant school and especially in
winter when snow spirits swirled across the highway and
followed me home and beautiful rich women in
cashmere sweaters drinking apple martinis wearing big
hats followed me with their eyes and even

the cops smiling and never mind when some of the
furniture in the parlor began to move (spirits being
disturbed) i didn't mind that or mourning doves on the
frozen solid telephone lines you see i loved my island

without you on it until one day at a small intimate dinner
party for five eating goat cheese drinking inexpensive
chilean wine and discussing the price of octopus in spain

i threw up.

STUCK ON THE BQE
THINKING ABOUT JIMMY SCHUYLER

sunday afternoon one thirty pm i'm unaccountably
crawling southbound on the BQE toward the
williamsburg bridge instead of flying along the highway
like a man ought to do, fly along a highway, if he was
driving anywhere else in america, but here we are in the
pothole capital of the world, driving over the rooftops of
Brooklyn stuck in traffic even though it's a sunday
afternoon in winter the economy is in shambles again,
the big rumbling engine of america has run out of gas
it's been abandoned on the side of the highway, america
is sitting on cinder blocks on the side of the road like it
used to do, like one of those cars back in the day,

abandoned on the cross bronx expressway by some
sucker from the suburbs and the local boys have
already pounced on it and stripped it down, and i'm
thinking how if this was back in the day i'd be living in
nyc with art critics and abstract expressionists i wouldn't
be pouncing on abandoned cars like the boys in the
south bronx, i mean if it was nineteen fifty something i'd
be drinking beer at the cedar tavern with jackson pollock
and franz klein, i'd be working at the front desk of
MOMA like frank o'hara, i would be cruising the streets
with crazy chester kallman staying with people in
Southampton making friends with wh auden and Harold
norse and fairfield porter i would be doing it like jimmy
schuyler

used to do it, i'd be back in the day, and the sexy trucks
would be rolling up second avenue for me, like they did
in schuyler's poem 'february,' just rolling away into the
sky like all the hot young lovers that rolled into and out
of jimmy schuyler's life, but i'm not jimmy i'm not jimmy
i'm not jimmy i'm not living back in the day I'm living in
the now even though it feels like february the way old
jimmy described it in his poem his very good poem
'february' with its tulips trying to open up and its women
jiggling babies in windows with their tight little eyes—no
it's not february it's march fifteenth, i'll be sixty years old

next week sixty! By the time jimmy schuyler was this old most of the important people in his life were dead, bunny, frank, jimmy lesoeur, he had diabetes the american academy of poets had elected him fellow they were handing that boy ten thousand dollars a year if you can believe that, ten thousand! all i ever get from those bastards is notices that i oughta be a member or else i was a member but now my membership

is about to expire and i'm wondering where are all the important and dead men in my life? what if i could get ten thousand dollars a year from the academy instead of paying them thirty five bucks? and how can a man even see the UN building the way jimmy schuyler did in that poem, because from where i'm sitting here on the BQE that building looks like a big bad box of american cereal to me, not a 'green wave in a violet sea,' which is a perfectly

good image but i mean what was old jimmy thinking about when he said that, what angle was he looking at that goddamn building from and was that sun or maybe smog in his eyes, what was he trying to say, i mean look at that terrible building! the UN building? i suppose there's some angle it doesn't look like an IBM card from, or a big ugly box of blind american kelloggs cornflakes, maybe from some angle it looks like a big damn keyhole

that if you find the right key and you jiggle it just right you might open the door to eternity—and i'm thinking they don't leave holes in the new york city skyline the way they used to, do they? They don't leave them there for very long, i mean, they just fill them up with something new, but then again maybe jimmy schuyler was on to something, maybe he could see something i can't see, maybe there would be a big hole in the NYC skyline if you took the UN building away, like death put a hole in the sky

the day it took jimmy schuyler away from the rest of us,
because after all a lot of people i know miss jimmy
schuyler a lot and they talk about him all the time, and
even though i never knew the man, i know them, so
sometimes i talk about him too

STOPPING FOR A PISS IN MISSOURI

the cross country bus stops unexpectedly on the side of the road and the driver gets up from his seat. the bus door opens and he steps out into the field. we are in missouri, he is going outside to take a leak in a field in the sun. he is a large man. you can see that even from this side of the bus. quite a bit larger than one might imagine! a woman across from me half gets up out of her seat to watch. she begins to complain but her companion tells her to shut it and she does. from the look of him standing there, his back to the bus in the tall grass, he looks to be about as wide as a bread delivery truck. any kind of panel truck, really. one that's been driven off the road and into some hasty bushes by some kids with nothing to do all day. they've borrowed it from a neighbor's driveway, filled it full of beer and musical instruments, and driven it down to this field full of sun and haze and buzzing insects. they've abandoned it in the sun for a few hours. they've walked indian file down a clandestine pathway only they know about. now they are relaxing down at a place over the hill where you and i can't see them. a place with a swim hole and a flat rock where young people go for smoking pot and some good old fashioned naked swimming, without being disturbed by cops or grownups.

from where i am sitting i can see the arc of the bus driver pissing; it looks like the st louis arch in the sun. i wonder if being a man with a field in missouri would be a nice kind of a man to be. the sun would feel good splashing on my arms and face. i could smell things growing all around me. things that are rich and alive. nothing like new york city. wheat or barley. clover. hay. honeybees. horses you could ride. a smoke shed you could keep for curing hams. i want to get out of the bus and look around at the real estate. i'm quite sure the bus driver wouldn't mind. from where i am sitting he looks like a decent man, i mean who notices a bus driver? he looks like a man who wouldn't turn around or stare over his left shoulder if one of the passengers was to happen to get out and have a look around while he's peeing. nice place for a picnic i could say, loud enough for only him and me to hear. he would notice but he wouldn't say anything, he's not like that. he would just keep on pissing.

after a long time the driver gets back on the bus. he takes his seat and closes the bus door and things go back to normal. everyone is relieved, you can hear the sound of it throughout the bus. people settling back into their seats, getting comfortable again. we're going to do that thing we have all gotten on this bus for. we're going to move forward. the bus bumps into gear, i would say the motion's between a nudge and a jolt. like being inside a small ancient shack on the side of a mountain in chile, a shack with a tin roof that has felt the earth move many times over and become used to it. a shack in chile, that is still standing in any weather. whenever the earth moves, that shack sways, but it never falls. as for the people inside, when the earth begins to shake they don't even get up out of bed anymore. they just go on making love to each other. sometimes he says to his friends, her? she's a field of arrowheads and rocks. it's like sticking it into a bag of razor blades. sometimes she says to her friends, him? he's one tired old rooster. like a rag you wouldn't put into your mouth unless you have got to put a stop to a toothache. that's just talk, they've become accustomed to their lives. when the earth moves, they hold on tight to each other and they rock with the motion. if they do that, they both loosen up. if they do that, their lovemaking goes quite a lot better. if they do that, it makes them both feel content about themselves and their present situation.

THERE'S A SHOT FOR THAT

the day after christmas is like any brutal morning in
winter only worse. it's like waking up on the floor of your
apartment blind or next to a blonde you hate or an
empty bottle of peppermint schnapps.

it's like being locked up with a professional clown who
has run out of new ways to be funny so he tips his
stupid red tricycle over again and again and again.

it's like two teams you don't care about playing football.
or a woman with big hair on television reporting the
news. or soggy unexplained underwear or a seventeen
hour kung fu movie marathon.

it's like sawdust in a man's mouth.

it's like deliberately shoving a wood splinter into your left
eye.

but there's a shot for all that.

i used to live with a woman who snorted pretty loud
when she laughed, there's a shot for that.

i used to walk like a fat man with short legs who knows
for sure he's going to miss the train to work and he
doesn't care, there's a shot for that too.

i used to feel like a toy dog with white fluffy hair shaved
legs and a rhinestone collar sitting in a rich woman's lap
who daydreams about getting in touch with his inner
rottweiler.

there's not a shot for that but i hear they're working on
one.

POPPIN' JOHNNY

i am on my way
i shoot through clouds
they are better than your jesus
heaven ain't just any heaven
it's my heaven and yes
i soar over apartments
i spit on your factories
they are irrelevant to me
i live up here, above wheat fields
and the pinetop mountain
i sparkle like the fourth of july
i am not like you
with your indecent necklaces
i am not like the others
with their home improvement lives
i fly the straight beeline
i do the big loop-di-loop
that's right i take to the sky
call me poppin' johnny!
i got wings like prairies
i got tail like barracudee
if you want to see me
go look up at the air
if you want to see me
go look where the birds go
and the sweet angels migrating
i have got no schoolbooks
no home by seven
and no particular woman
who calls herself mine
heaven is not my enemy
stars do not undo my eyes
as for this blasted earth of yours
it will never drag me down

ABOUT GEORGE WALLACE

George Wallace (AB, MPH, MFA) is an award winning poet and journalist from New York who has performed his work across America and in Europe. Author of 18 chapbooks of poetry, he has served as editor of Poetrybay (www.poetrybay.com), an online poetry magazine archived and distributed worldwide by Stanford University through its LOCKSS program; also Long Island Quarterly, Walt's Corner and other electronic and hard copy publications. A former Peace Corps Volunteer, USAF Medical Officer and Community Health Organizer, he is winner of the CW Post Poetry Prize and the Poetry Kit Best Book award. Wallace is listed by Poets & Writers, is a member of PEN-American and the Academy of American Poets, and is host of a monthly poetry series at the Bowery Poetry Club, at the Huntington Poetry Barn and other locations. In 2003, he was named first Poet Laureate for Suffolk County, NY. In 2007 he was named a "Next Generation Beat" by the Lowell Celebrates Kerouac festival committee.

ALSO ON
THREE ROOMS PRESS

POETRY

by Peter Carlaftes
Drive By Brooding
I Canto Cantos
Nightclub Confidential
Progressive Shots
Sheer Bardom
The Bar Essentials

by Ryan Buynak
Enjoy the Regrets
Yo Quiero Mas Sangre

by Joie Cook
When Night Salutes the Dawn

by Kathi Georges
Bred for Distance
Punk Rock Journal
Slow Dance at 120 Beats a Minute

by Karen Hildebrand
One Foot Out the Door

by Dominique Lowell
Sit Yr Ass Down or You Ain't gettin no Burger King

by Jane Ormerod
Recreational Vehicles on Fire

by Susan Scutti
We Are Related

by Jackie Sheeler
to[o] long

by The Bass Player from Hand Job
Splitting Hairs

by Angelo Vergo
Praise for What Remains

PLAYS

by Madeline Artenberg & Karen Hildebrand
The Old In-and-Out

by Larry Myers
Mary Anderson's Encore
Twitter Theater

To order, please email threeroomspress@mac.com

THREE ROOMS PRESS *New York*
www.threeroomspress.blogspot.com
threeroomspress@mac.com

CPSIA information can be obtained
at www.ICGtesting.com
Printed in the USA
LVOW12s1248310518
579060LV00001B/15/P